Fire Morels For Profit

Doris Price

ISBN: 1501033662
ISBN-13: 9781501033667

DEDICATION

To all future Mushroom pickers.
To your success and dedication to "Shrooming"

What readers are saying:
Thanks Doris for this informative book. It really helped me figure out
where the morels were and how to prepare them for the buyers. That was
quite an experience. Looking forward to next years' hunting.
Heather Bucchose Quesnel, BC, Now a confirmed mushroom picker.

So glad I had your book—it helped to identify the "Brain" morel and to
decide where to look for the fire morels. They are so hard to see, hiding in
the leaves. But as you say " where there is one there is many". It is so
exciting when you do finally find them peeking through the leaves.
Kathy Hawley, Vanderhoof BC a newcomer to picking fire morels

CONTENTS

Dear Reader,

I got the idea for writing this booklet while standing in line forever the buyer patiently explained to pickers what he wanted. He sorted through each basket and actually sent people away to re-clean their mushroom or refused to buy because what was offered was too wet, crushed or dirty. So I consulted a few very experienced pickers and heeded the complaints of the buyers. The result was the following booklet.

Visit my website at http://firemorelsforprofit.com/ for mushroom tips and watch a video **Morel Mushroom GrowingTimeline**.

Doris Price

Doris Price

1 INTRODUCTION

Few things compare to the thrill of poking through the woods, grass, and underbrush in search of this tasty little morsel. When you do find them chances are that there will be more than one. The reason for this is that fungi tend to have an underground "root" system that is normally there but relies on the proper conditions to flourish.

Moisture, temperature and other factors dictate whether they will "pop" and when. A link has been observed between wildfires one year and morel mushroom fruiting the following spring. There may also be a link between morels and extensive tree mortality from insect epidemics (for example, the mountain pine beetle).

Fire Morels are renowned for their earthy taste and pleasing texture, the morel is a rare delicacy prized by chefs and mushroom hunters alike. Most of the Canadian mushrooms are exported to French and European restaurants.

Morels are one of the few mushrooms associated with wildfire in British Columbia forests.

Wild morels from British Columbia forests comprise a multi-million-dollar non-timber forest products industry. My book Fire Morels for Profit explains how to pick the morel so that buyers will give top dollar, what equipment is needed and where to find picking spots.

As an avid, seasoned mushroom picker, I wanted to share my experience and help mushroom-pickers start picking the right way without having the heartache of having mushrooms discarded by buyers because they were not picked correctly

2 THINGS TO CONSIDER

Picking fire morels to earn wages is hard and dirty work.

There's a lot of walking, climbing and the key word here is dirty. The ash will go right through your clothes. It will be in your nose, ears and into places no one wants to disclose. But beware picking Fire Morels is addictive. Commonly known as Mushroom Fever.

In good physical shape?

Great, but remember your body will find a lot of muscles you didn't know you had but if you survive the first few days you'll toughen up.
Still willing to try?

Then here are a few hints to launch your new endeavor.

Taking a break to watch the sun set
.

3 THINGS TO CONSIDER

Condition of Fire Burn

There are many factors that will decide how well you'll do.

First how deep the fire burned, was there enough moisture at the right time, a few sunny days to warm up the soil and start them growing and last but not least a patch where no one else has picked.

What you are looking for is a 1 year old burn. One that is burnt deep and not just a flash fire over the top. The mushroom spore is already in the ground waiting for the right conditions. The morel spore could have been waiting there 25 years or more. Just depends on when the area last had a fire. When the soil reaches 50 degrees Fahrenheit the mushrooms will begin to grow..

Bear Chaser

4 PIGS EARS

A good indication that conditions are right is when Pigs Ears are growing in the area and are about one-half inch in size. The first crop starts on the Eastern slopes in the low ground. As the weather warms up they will start to grow on the Southern slopes and finally progress to the Western slopes.

Pigs Ears.

.

5 FALSE MORELS

There are many types of true morels but beware of picking false morels. A true morel is hollow inside. The false morel is solid and if you were to cut it open you would see the flesh inside is wrinkled. They don't show up very often and the buyer will just throw them out

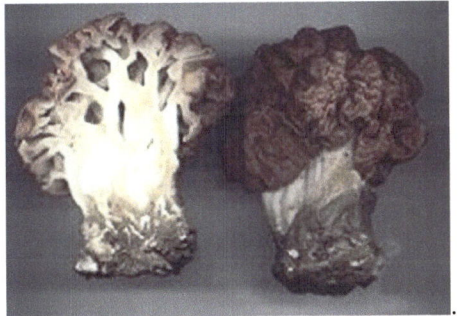

False Morels

True Morel

6 BRAIN MUSHROOM

Another type of false morel is the Brain mushroom

This one can be a cash crop. It actually looks like a large brain and can run from rust, brown or black in color. It grows in logging sites. Look for slashes where the needles on the downed trees have turned red. When the snow and rain drove the needles into the soil it turned the natural morels into the Brain mushroom. They can grow to a very large size. If you live in an area that has been logged, check for a buyer. The Brain mushroom start appearing just before the natural morels do. A Brain mushroom is not a table mushroom. The buyer will dry them and ship them overseas.

Picking Brain for a little extra cash is a great way to get a little fresh air and exercise even if you don't get rich.

Pack them into your pails and baskets very carefully. They crumble easily.

Never transport them in an enclosed vehicle. They smell a lot like aircraft fuel. You'll get a headache.

A word of warning do not pick mushrooms in Provincial or Federal Parks. You will receive a heavy fine if you do.

Yellow Morels

The true morels, is an edible mushrooms.. These distinctive mushrooms appear honeycomb-like in that the upper portion is composed of a network of ridges with pits between them. Morels are hunted by thousands of people every year simply for their taste and the joy of the hunt.. All types of morels may grow abundantly in forests which have been burned by a forest fire with black morels at the start of the season, followed by the yellows, greys and greens. The mechanism for this behavior is not well known,] but appears to be related to both the death of trees and the removal of organic material on the forest

7 HOME CAMPS AND OTHER SUPPLIES

Now that you have planned where to go lets discuss what you'll need.

Some people travel in motor homes, campers or just tent it. I have even seen frames built out of poles and covered with tarps. Quite roomy in my mind. The usual camping gear doesn't need to be discussed I'm sure.

Picking your camp will depend upon the individual.

If you like a lot of people there are usually camp sites around some buyers. You'll meet lots of interesting people from far and wide.

Privacy is more our thing so we find a spot close to running water that is easily accessible without any neighbours.

Some buyers set up **showers** by their stations. Some showers are complimentary and others are charged for. Myself, I take along a solar shower bag found in any department store sports center.

Just fill it full of water and hang it in the sun and by the time you return from picking you will have enough warm water for several showers. I find two or three close trees and wrap a tarp around them for a shower stall. Of course if it's not sunny you'll have to heat the water yourself and fill it up. Some brave individuals bath in streams or lakes but I like warm water thank you.

camping in luxury

8 MUSHROOM CARRYING EQUIPMENT

You will need **5 gallon pails** to pick in.

Drill holes in the bottom and even up the sides if you can to let moisture out. Make sure you have a cover for your pails. Dirt and leaves etc. will make cleaning the mushrooms harder. Just cut a slit in the top so you can pop your mushrooms in. A cover will also help protect your find if you get caught in the rain. You definitely don't want your mushrooms to get wet.

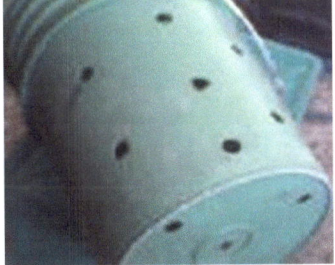

A **packboard** with a bench to hold baskets will help you carry out your treasure..

The **baskets and lids** you'll get from the buyer. You will need twist ties to hold the lids on. You wouldn't want to spill the results of your hard work. The best picking is had by out-walking as many other pickers as you can. Returning to your vehicle with your mushrooms often is not feasible. You can strap several baskets to the pack board and carry two 5 gallon pails in your hands..

A **sharp paring knife** or even a plastic one in a pinch is a must. Tie a bright ribbon around the handle. You have no idea how hard it is to find your knife once you've dropped it. The buyer wants the stems cut with a quarter inch stem and no dirt. Your mushrooms should be clean enough to eat. Some people pinch the mushrooms off but it looks untidy and the idea is to present the best looking product. Besides you'll get a stain that will take at least 6 weeks to wear off.

Good **hiking shoes** will help you conserve your energy. I've picked in athletic shoes with good traction. Remember, you are going to be hiking and most likely climbing in some rough and slippery terrain.

Take **comfortable clothes** that you can throw away at the end of the season. I go to the thrift shops. Wear shirts with long sleeves. They may save you from sunburn, nasty scratches and of course bug bites.

Don't forget the sunscreen and mosquito repellent

9 WHERE TO FIND MUSHROOM BUYERS

Some mushroom buyers are in town close to the burn site and but most are set up along the roads leading to the burn. Most buyers set up a station every afternoon about 4 o'clock and others make permanent camps. As the season gets off to a good start there are usually a lot of buyers. You can't miss them. Signs on the roads saying **"Shroom Buyer"**. Check out the buyers. Most are helpful and honest and only once did we find one that had a quarter on his scales. He was soon out of business. Find out how much they are paying per pound. If their quotas aren't filled yet they can be competitive

Prices depend on the market.

Remember the mushrooms in the United States have to come in first, they are the first to bloom then the weather starts to warm up in Canada around the spring season, which runs from Mid-April to Mid-June and collectors mostly search for the edible ones in the woods within this brief period. As the market becomes flooded the prices will go down.

Buyers are usually very friendly and will ask you for your name. One buyer told me she had an awful lot of country and western singers picking and among them was Johnny Cash!

Mushroom Buyers

If you find a small burn and there are no buyers, it may pay you to haul your mushrooms to the nearest big burn where the buyers are. The lack of competition usually makes up for the cost of gas. When we checked out an area and found out it was good, we had to travel nearly 2 hours to a buyer. We told the buyer about it and they sent someone to set-up a buying station and of course brought more pickers with them.

Some buyers buy for the fresh market and some dry them. We try to dry about 25% of our pick. Then hold them in reserve to sell at the beginning of the next season when prices are high. You should be able to find detailed information about setting up a dryer and the care of the dried product on the Internet if you are so inclined

Black Morels BC Forest

.

10 FINAL WORDS OF WISDOM

I got the idea for writing this booklet while standing in line forever at a buyers station. Hot, dirty, tired and hungry I watched while the buyer patiently explained to pickers what he wanted. He sorted through each basket and actually sent away people to re-clean their mushrooms or refused to buy because what was offered was too wet, crushed or dirty.

The buyers job begins when the picker hunts a bath and a hot meal. What they bought has to be sorted, loaded, and delivered to the nearest airport for delivery to the nearest major city for the fresh market or loaded into the driers which have to be checked periodically during the night. A lot of buyers look a little frayed around the edges by the end of the season.

I hope I have given you good advice. Good luck. Good picking and I'll see you in the burn.

Fire Burn

Doris Price

11 MUSHROOM JOURNAL

I found having a journal to record my ramblings and success at picking was a relaxing end to my day. I have included a journal here

Just remember where there is one there is many...

Date:
Weather:
Location:

I'd rather be shroomin'

Date:
Weather:
Location:

Got shroom?

Date:
Weather:
Location:

Another Mushroom Day

Date:
Weather:
Location:

Shrooming Along

Date:
Weather:
Location:

My Shrooms

Date:
Weather:
Location:

More shrooms'

Date:
Weather:
Location:

Date:
Weather:
Location:

ABOUT THE AUTHOR

Doris has always found time to help others by sharing her knowledge and sense of fun. One more opportunity presented itself while in the Northern Climes of BC, hunting and picking fire morels.

As an avid, seasoned mushroom picker, Doris wanted to share her experience and help mushroom-pickers start picking the right way without having the heartache of having mushrooms discarded by buyers because they were not picked correctly.

Apart from enjoying the outdoors, camping and hunting Fire Morels, Doris is an avid RedHat Lady. She belongs to the Prince George, BC chapter. She recently went on a tour by VIA rail to Prince Rupert to visit the local RedHat Ladies there.